0500001049709 2

D1524371

Rats

by Joanne Mattern

BELLWETHER MEDIA • MINNEAPOLIS, MN

Blastoff! Readers are carefully developed by literacy experts to build reading stamina and move students toward fluency by combining standards-based content with developmentally appropriate text.

Level 1 provides the most support through repetition of high-frequency words, light text, predictable sentence patterns, and strong visual support.

Level 2 offers early readers a bit more challenge through varied sentences, increased text load, and text-supportive special features.

Level 3 advances early-fluent readers toward fluency through increased text load, less reliance on photos, advancing concepts, longer sentences, and more complex special features.

★ **Blastoff! Universe**

Reading Level

Grade **K**

Grades **1–3**

Grade **4**

This edition first published in 2021 by Bellwether Media, Inc.

No part of this publication may be reproduced in whole or in part without written permission of the publisher. For information regarding permission, write to Bellwether Media, Inc., Attention: Permissions Department, 6012 Blue Circle Drive, Minnetonka, MN 55343.

Library of Congress Cataloging-in-Publication Data

Names: Mattern, Joanne, 1963- author.
Title: Rats / by Joanne Mattern.
Description: Minneapolis, MN : Bellwether Media, 2021. | Series: Blastoff! readers: the world's smartest animals | Includes bibliographical references and index. | Audience: Ages 5-8 | Audience: Grades 2-3 | Summary: "Simple text and full-color photography introduce beginning readers to rats. Developed by literacy experts for students in kindergarten through third grade"-- Provided by publisher.
Identifiers: LCCN 2019059336 (print) | LCCN 2019059337 (ebook) | ISBN 9781644872420 (library binding) | ISBN 9781681037059 (ebook)
Subjects: LCSH: Rats--Behavior--Juvenile literature. | Animal intelligence--Juvenile literature.
Classification: LCC QL737.R666 M29 2021 (print) | LCC QL737.R666 (ebook) | DDC 599.35156--dc23
LC record available at https://lccn.loc.gov/2019059336
LC ebook record available at https://lccn.loc.gov/2019059337

Editor: Betsy Rathburn   Designer: Jeffrey Kollock

Printed in the United States of America, North Mankato, MN.

Table of Contents

Smart Rodents

Rats are small **mammals**. They are part of the **rodent** family. Mice and squirrels are part of this family, too.

These critters live all over the world! Some live in the wild. Others are kept as pets.

Rats are very **social**. In the wild, they live in nests with several other rats. There are often many nests in one place!

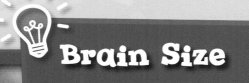

Brain Size

about
1,400
grams

human

about
2
grams

rat

As pets, rats do best when they have a friend.

Smart and Skilled

Rats use **intelligence** to survive in the wild. They make sounds to **communicate** with other rats.

Some rats also communicate with **body language**. They swish their tails to show they are upset!

Rats have good memories. They can remember places they have been before.

They remember past animals, too. They know if animals they have seen before are dangerous!

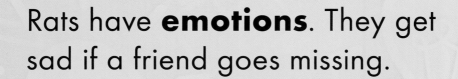

Rats have **emotions**. They get sad if a friend goes missing.

They have **empathy**, too. They often show **distress** if they see other distressed rats!

Wild rats sometimes get stuck in traps. But they are good problem-solvers. They often escape!

Rat Skills

communicates

has emotions

solves problems

remembers well

burrow

Rats escape **predators**, too. Their **burrows** often have many entrance holes. If danger is near, they leave through another hole.

Learning About Rats

Scientists study how rats learn. They train rats to run through mazes. They also teach rats tricks. Rats get treats when they learn new tricks.

Rat Study

Question

Do rats care about each other?

Process

1. Two rats were kept together for a few weeks.

2. One rat was placed alone in a cage. It got very upset.

3. Another cage held chocolate chips.

4. The second rat could choose to free the trapped rat or eat the chocolate.

What Happened?

- The rat chose to free the trapped rat instead of rewarding itself with chocolate.

Answer

- Rats care about each other and will help each other.

Many of the smartest animals use tools. Scientists tested whether rats can learn to use tools.

Amazing Rats

Name
- University of Richmond rats

Date
- 2019

Famous For
- Lab rats learned to drive tiny cars
- Driving cars helped the rats relax

In one **experiment**, rats were trained to use hooks. They pulled chocolate cereal into their cages!

People mostly study **lab** rats.
But pet rats learn, too.
Owners teach them tricks.

These intelligent animals are among the smartest in the world!

Glossary

body language—movements of the body that communicate thoughts and feelings

burrows—holes or tunnels that some animals use for homes

communicate—to share thoughts and feelings using sounds, faces, and actions

distress—fear or pain

emotions—feelings

empathy—the ability to understand the thoughts, feelings, and experiences of others

experiment—a test used to try new ideas or answer questions

intelligence—the ability to learn or understand

lab—a place where scientists research

mammals—warm-blooded animals that have backbones and feed their young milk

predators—animals that hunt other animals for food

rodent—related to small animals that gnaw on their food

social—marked by having many relationships with others

To Learn More

AT THE LIBRARY

Hansen, Grace. *Rats*. Minneapolis, Minn.: Abdo Kids, 2016.

Kenney, Karen Latchana. *Super Rats*. Minneapolis, Minn.: Jump!, 2018.

Polinsky, Paige V. *My Pet Rat*. Minneapolis, Minn.: Bellwether Media, 2020.

ON THE WEB

FACTSURFER

Factsurfer.com gives you a safe, fun way to find more information.

1. Go to www.factsurfer.com.

2. Enter "rats" into the search box and click 🔍.

3. Select your book cover to see a list of related content.

23

Index

The images in this book are reproduced through the courtesy of: torook, front cover, p. 1; Eric Isselee, pp. 3, 14; TashaBubo, pp. 4, 5; Shaganart, p. 5; Liukov, pp. 6, 7; Florian Bott, pp. 8, 9; Alan Tunnicliffe, p. 9; Bilal Kocabas, p. 10; scooperdigital, pp. 10, 11; JuliLeo, pp. 12, 13; LankaP, p. 13; Bill Gozansky/ Alamy, pp. 14, 15; BonkersAboutScience/ Alamy, p. 16; Bilanol, p. 16; ZaZa Studio, p. 17; Pakhnyushchy, p. 17; University of Richmond, p. 18; Kirill Kurashov, pp. 18, 19; lilechik-h, pp. 20, 21; Maksymenko Nataliia, p. 23.